FOUR FACES of a WORSHIPPER

Andrew Allans Mutambo

FOUR FACES OF A WORSHIPPER

Rivendell Publishing
www.rivendellpublishing.com

ORGINAL LAYOUT DESIGN & PRINT:
Anthony Saint
+254 722 102232/ +256 779
982377 tony.saint30@gmail.com

To order copies online visit:
www.andrewmutambo.com

To schedule a speaking engagement or for more information contact:

Andrew Mutambo

P.O BOX 22292

KAMPALA, UGANDA.

U.S. Line: 1-804-601-0394

Ugandan Line: (256)-772-404389

Email: andymutts@gmail.com

Dedication

This manuscript, being my first publication, is dedicated to the Almighty God who saved and called me by his grace to be his mouthpiece in this generation. May every person who undertakes to read this book be inspired to seek out their God given place of worship and seize the moment. Worship is the heart-beat of God. Rallying people behind this cause is my purposed destiny.

I also dedicate this book to my parents who from a tender age showed me the religious pathway of life. Attending church every Sunday morning was a way of life in our family. We as children looked forward to this day. This consistency helped form discipline in me and prepared me for a lifetime of service to a higher Power. I am what I am because of godly parents and a fear of God in our family. Dad and Mum, am thankful to God for you.

Acknowledgement

I wish to express my heartfelt gratitude to my family and Church folk whose love, support and prayers have been an inspiration and encouragement in fulfilling the tasks God has entrusted me with. You are sails of my yacht.

Foreword by Harold Bare

My pastoral experience has now exceeded 35 years. Scores of missionaries have been a intimate part of my life. Personal encounters with missionaries have been via Covenant Church, mine and Laila's home, or in more distant places, e.g., conferences, seminars, and native lands.

Andrew came into our lives via someone's recommendation. He stayed in our home. We have spent long hours talking about ministry, his love for ministry, and his desire and ability to make a significant contribution to the Kingdom of God. Andrew is one of the most culturally adaptable missionaries of my acquaintance. He is a thinker outside the box.

His treatise regarding worship and the place of music in worship is a contribution to be read and appreciated. It provokes thoughtful contemplation and encouragement to make sure that fads and fashions are not being substituted for biblical worship. Andrew via this writing makes clear that activities that do not exalt Our Glorious Heav-

enly Father fail. Our sole purpose for existence and worship is exaltation!

Bishop Harold L. Bare, Sr., Ph.D.
Senior Pastor,
Covenant Church,
Charlottesville, Virginia, USA.

Foreword by Thurlow Switzer

Andrew Mutambo has written an inspiring and vivid account about worship, drawing metaphors from the Four Living Creatures described in Ezekiel 1:10. Passionate about the reality of worship before a Holy God, Andrew communicates that passion page after page.

Worship must be the first and highest priority for the Church of Jesus Christ. Much of the church is worshipping at a mediocre level, quite passive before the Lord, seldom entering into the Holy of Holies corporately, where the presence of God hovers over the congregation and the power of God is felt deeply, personally, and intimately. Andrew captures the reality and empowerment that is derived from God's presence.

Having heard in person one of these chapters communicated in our congregation when the congregants were stirred to respond in passionate worship, I was no less stirred by reading the same message in print. Read and note the power of the metaphors in this excellent book

and reflect on the scriptures. You will experience trans-
formation and motivation in your personal worship of
God. This book is a cutting-edge message needed afresh
by our generation. Multiple copies should be ordered and
the book used for small group discussions. Andrew Mutambo is a rising servant to the Body of Christ, one who
lives out and practices what he encourages.

Apostle Thurlow J. Switzer
Living Grace Ministries,
Montgomery Village, MD, USA
www.lgmweb.org

Appreciation

I extend my sincere thanks to Dr. Bill Jackson, retired professor of the University of Virginia for the time put in editing my manuscript.

My thanks as well go to Dr. Harold Bare for the continuous fatherly advice he gives to me, Apostle Thurlow Switzer and Pastor Geronimo Aguilar for their forewords. Pastor Danny Mbako, thanks for being a close friend who has always offered cutting edge advice and counsel.

Preface

Through my travels, I have chanced to meet and interact with people of diverse social and cultural backgrounds, participated in home cell meetings, public worship gatherings, church services, the list goes on. My experiences have revealed that to a great extent, little is known or understood about worship or its ministration. A cross section of well intentioned religious folks perceive it as an act of attending mass or singing a couple of hymnal songs on a given Sunday or Saturday morning, others as listening to and enjoying a church band or choir performing. Many approach it in a casual mood and like a passing wind hardly embrace its effects and sway.

To better understand the mystery of worship, one has to retrace its footsteps to the story of creation. God's intended purpose for creating man was fellowship. He created a perfect place, Eden. Eden means "pleasurable and delightsome." In this environment, He would meet with man. Eden was depictive of God's presence. In this atmosphere, man basked and 'intercoursed' with his creator on a continuous basis. At his fall, the intimacy was forfeited and man was banned from God's presence.

Throughout history, humankind has struggled and sought to replace or substitute for this fellowship through worship of angels, sun, moon, stars, animals, spirit mediums, man-made idols, New age ideology, the list goes on. The scriptures are emphatic about the purpose of our creation.

Isaiah 43:7 - *Even every one that is called by my name: for I have created him for my glory, I have formed him; yea, I have made him.*

In this book, I attempt to unravel the inscrutability of the four living creatures that stand 24/7 in the midst of the throne of His majesty. They are a perfect representation of what Eden was meant to be, a place where God's will was enshrined. Come with me as I chant the course of Man's designed pursuit of and ultimate destiny with his creator!

Ezekiel 1:10 - *As for the likeness of their faces, they four had the face of a man, and the face of a lion, on the right side: and they four had the face of an ox on the left side; they four also had the face of an eagle.*

Revelations 4:7 - *And the first beast was like a lion, and the second beast like a calf, and the third beast had a face as a man, and the fourth beast was like a flying eagle.*

Table of Contents

Chapter One

FACE OF A LION

When Satan forfeited his role as the arch-angel, charged with leading the heavenly host in venerating God, the cherubim were instituted. These four living creatures centered in the 'throne-circle' night and day pay homage to the Ancient of Days crying; holy, holy, holy is the Lord God Almighty, AND the rest of the celestial beings, the twenty four elders burst into a heavenly orchestra in response to this antiphonal call. Each one of these creatures has a shape and facial component of great spiritual symbolism. In them, a total package of worship is assembled.

Let us set in motion our first chapter by exploring the

spiritual significance of the Lion face and creature vis-a-vis worship, comparing natural facts with biblical truth.

1. Female lions are known to roar to protect their cubs from external males trying to infiltrate the pride, by calling nearby females to help defend her young OR calling the resident male lion to confront any encroaching male. The purpose of the encroacher is to overthrow the current dynasty and kill all the cubs of the incumbent male lion.

As female lions go into 'protective mode' for their young by roaring, our roar as the bride of Christ is in our worship. When we begin roaring through worship, the spiritual atmosphere around us is ignited; awareness comes afloat. This sends a prophetic signal to the rest of the pride (spiritual gathering) to arise to our God-given position and withstand our aggressor. This is evidenced in the kind of songs the Spirit of God puts on the hearts of His people during a worship moment. Sometimes they are songs that propel us into spiritual combat as we praise Him!

Worship is a prophetic call. It stirs and stimulates hearts

towards a particular goal. Worship is also an offensive tool, a weapon of our warfare. The more we roar in our worship, the more divine wrath and fear is instilled in our intruder's path, causing him to scurry away as we establish our dominance over the territory and domain that belongs to us. Sickness, poverty, death and every baggage the enemy would have thought to bring in to our midst, is obliterated and withstood, as we roar in our worship!

The devil will through your lifetime try to encroach on what is yours. Sitting back and crying foul waiting for God to show up will not deter him from his purpose. It is not until the female lion who has spotted the intruder roars against him, that the spiritual ambiance comes alive. Child of God it is time to roar!

 This roar also arouses Christ, the resident male lion, the Lion of Judah, to take his place in our midst. There are things God will NOT do or respond to except H is people invoke him. As we recognize H is rule and role through our worship, He steps in and exerts HIS influence over His domain, which domain we are. We are his offspring. His special people. On a consistent basis our worship-roar should echo, "Let God arise and His enemies be scattered". When we do so, without a doubt He will arise!

Proverbs 19:12 - *The king's wrath is as the roaring of a lion; but his favor is as dew upon the grass.*

Proverbs 20:2 - *The fear of a king is as the roaring of a lion: whoso provoketh him to anger sinneth against his own soul.*

2. Resident males roar at night, to announce their presence, or else have smelled an intruder lion and are warning them off. When a lion roars, it can do so with enough force to raise a cloud of dust, instill great fear in any prey AND raise the hairs on a humans head. It is said that a lion's roar can be heard 5 miles (8 km) away on a still night.

God has inured his intervention on the action of his people. Christ's voice (symbolized by the return roar from the resident male lion) to His church comes to ensure His protection and affirm His lordship and kingship over us. In quintessence worship activates the voice of God upon your life. This voice though still and soft comes and goes forth into the innermost and furthermost recesses of our

lives with sufficient power and authority to undo every diabolic work and assert His sovereignty and establish His kingdom.

> **Amos 3:8** - *The lion hath roared, who will not fear? the Lord GOD hath spoken, who can but prophesy?*

> **Hosea 11:10** - *They shall walk after the LORD: he shall roar like a lion: when he shall roar, then the children shall tremble from the west.*

It's also important to note that, the 'noise' of our worship as seen in the scriptural reference below, is equated to the voice of the almighty. Worship is the highest form of spiritual intercourse cultivated in 'high-places'. In these moments of intense fellowship with God, the sweet sound of our voices is embalmed and amplified with dunamis... spiritual power. On the face of it, as you make melody and worship, you may not notice, but behind the scenes, in the un-seen world, the enemy sees, hears and recognizes what is going on!

That is why in periods of intense worship, it's important

to be Perceptive and recognizant, and to continuously roll with the momentum of praise and adoration emanating from your heart and lips as you keep stretching your wings of worship, carrying the glory of God into every area of your life. The sound of true worship is surely as powerful as his voice!

> **Ezekiel 1:24 -** *And when they went, I heard the noise of their wings, like the noise of great waters, as the voice of the Almighty, the voice of speech, as the noise of an host: when they stood, they let down their wings.*

3. The fore-body of a lion is very powerfully built enabling it to deliver blows with its forepaws heavy enough to break a zebra's back. Compared to the tiger who is a fast jabber, the lion is the heavy weight in the cat family. In an ideal match, a lion will outmatch a tiger in a contest, knocking it off balance.

Analogously, the way we have been formed and fashioned in the image of God is unique! Our spiritual physique like the lion, enables us to exert such spiritual power and prowess as to give us mastery over our adversary.

The very members of our spiritual/physical bodies , i.e. hands, tongue and feet , when fully employed in moments of adoration become effective weaponry of victory. The lifting up of holy hands, the bellowing sounds that come from our lips/tongues and the very posture of kneeling, prostration or standing on our feet in reverent praise.... all give testimony to this immense armory we have.

In worship, every member that necessitates motion is vital. When we employ these tools, (hands, feet, tongue, etc) to their fullest, we begin 'creating' with our tongue, partaking with our hands and possessing with our feet what is duly ours, similar to the way a lion uses its teeth, paws and shoulder power to outwit its foe. " Bless the LORD, O my soul: and all that is within me, bless his holy name." (Psalms 103:1).

Daniel 6:24 - *And the king commanded, and they brought those men which had accused Daniel, and they cast them into the den of lions, them, their children, and their wives; and the lions had the mastery of them, and brake all their bones in pieces or ever they came at the bottom of the den.*

Proverbs 30:30 - *A lion which is strongest among beasts, and turneth not away for any.*

4. Females do most of the hunting. Males will eat first, then the females. The male, big, strong and clumsy, with a big mane, is less-adept as a hunter. Notwithstanding, the male can, by virtue of his size, easily kill a prey animal the females are struggling with. Male lions are still formidable hunters. When patrolling and guarding their territory, they will often hunt for themselves.

Listen carefully my friend to this spiritual truth. When the kill has been made by the females, the male takes its turn to eat first. In like manner, before we can think of enjoying and partaking the constant and continuous opportunities, blessings and victories that come to us on a day to day basis, Jesus as the male Lion and Lord SHOULD get the glory first!

It is mandatory for us to give Him the praise and adoration...symbolic of our first fruits to him. As the male lion is allowed to partake first of the kill, we purposely serve him before we serve our selves of any blessings due to us. We do it through our testimonies, praise reports,

tithes, thanksgiving and free will offerings. Because as the protector of the 'pride,' behind the scenes, HE forever watches over and fights for us invidiously. Make no mistake beloved, God shares his glory with no other. The day you fail to acknowledge him for the things done and received, that will be the beginning of your serving mammon. Elohim is a jealous God!

> **Isaiah 31:4** - *For thus hath the LORD spoken unto me, Like as the lion and the young lion roaring on his prey, when a multitude of shepherds is called forth against him, he will not be afraid of their voice, nor abase himself for the noise of them: so shall the LORD of hosts come down to fight for mount Zion, and for the hill thereof.*

5. Lions do their hunting in the night and morning. They do not chew but swallow their food in chunks. They mostly kill by suffocation, biting on the victim's throat, clamping the victims mouth and crushing the windpipe. It is common for the other lions to open the abdomen and begin eating while the animal is still being suffocated. This often kills the animal faster than the suffocation does. An adult will typically eat 40 pounds (18 Kg.) of meat at a time, with reports of as much as 75 pounds (34 Kg.) con-

sumed in one sitting.

Genuine worship produces such a craving and insatiable thirst for God that makes you want to love Him more, hold fast to Him and gullibly partake more of His presence and glory, unhindered and unabated. As a lion perceives and partakes of its prey, we too should stir up the bowels of our love to the point where nothing at a point in time matters, but more and more of Him and less and less of us till we are drenched in his presence and overwhelmed with his sovereignty. If and when Christians shall conjure this attitude as they prepare for a worship time with God, we are bound to see and experience divine visitations of the glory of God in our meetings on an unprecedented level.

> **Micah 5:8** - *And the remnant of Jacob shall be among the Gentiles in the midst of many people as a lion among the beasts of the forest, as a young lion among the flocks of sheep: who, if he go through, both treadeth down, and teareth in pieces, and none can deliver.*

6. Lions live in family structures consisting typically of

4-20 females with their cubs, and two or three males , which is the best situation for long-term survival. All of the females in the pride are related to one another, and the young cubs are usually of the pride male(s). Lions also rub each other in greeting. The rubbing can be quite vigorous and forceful. One person who raises lions suffered two broken ribs from a particularly intense rub she received in affection! This rubbing releases a scent which serves the purpose of bonding or belonging, and the other lions will relish this mark.

As much as worship is more of a personal nature, corporate¬worship is essential for any Christian. The scriptures in paraphrase say, " forsake not the habit of getting together for fellowship."This practice of communal worship releases an intensity of warmth and belonging that impacts a believer and assembly of believers. When the early church got together to pray and break bread, from house to house with singleness of heart, there was edification and growth. God honors unity because it releases a fresh atmosphere. Unified worship is uplifting, transformational and restorational, producing spontaneous life change. We can recall moments when God touched an aspect of our lives through a collective gathering. We should not substitute for these moments a

self made church service behind a television set or listening to a radio when we have the ability to make it to a traditional church service. We miss out on a great deal because of the attitudes we carry to a church service OR by absenting ourselves from one. Unified worship unleashes heavenly dew enough for everyone to be ministered to!

2 Chronicles 5:13 - *It came even to pass, as the trumpeters and singers were as one, to make one sound to be heard in praising and thanking the LORD; and when they lifted up their voice with the trumpets and cymbals and instruments of musick, and praised the LORD, saying, For he is good; for his mercy endureth for ever: that then the house was filled with a cloud, even the house of the LORD;*

2 Chronicles 5:14 - *So that the priests could not stand to minister by reason of the cloud: for the glory of the LORD had filled the house of God.*

Chapter Two

FACE OF AN OX

Each of the four cherubim had the face of an Ox. In much of the traditional and bucolic settings of the far east and African peninsula, the ox/bullock is still used to plough the fields in preparation for a sowing season. The fields are often a good stretch in breadth and length. But this animal, faithful to its owner, will plow for long hours day long. The service of this ox symbolizes devotion. This devotion is in its traditional use as a 'beast of burden.' In addition, the ox is the largest domesticated and edible animal...at least for most of the world. In the old testament economy, it was considered the ultimate sacrificial offering a person could present before the Lord. With regard

to worship, this living creature, the ox, is representative of our undying devotion and wholesome sacrifice to God. True worship entails giving our whole and all to God.

Romans 12:1 - *I beseech you therefore, brethren, by the mercies of God, that ye present your bodies a living sacrifice, holy, acceptable unto God, which is your reasonable service.*

We cannot break through the veil of our flesh to access the divine presence except we are willing to let go the weights and sin that beset us. In so doing, we are sacrificing and evidencing our devotion to God.

Jeremiah 31:18 - *I have surely heard Ephraim bemoaning himself thus; Thou hast chastised me, and I was chastised, as a bullock unaccustomed to the yoke: turn thou me, and I shall be turned; for thou art the LORD my God.*

Let us examine the old covenant system of worship in the first chapter of the book Leviticus to help us understand

the parallel and draw concepts applicable to our present day setting of worship.

Leviticus 1:1- *And the LORD called unto Moses, and spake unto him out of the tabernacle of the congregation, saying,*

Leviticus 1:2 - *Speak unto the children of Israel, and say unto them, If any man of you bring an offering unto the LORD, ye shall bring your offering of the cattle, even of the herd, and of the flock.*

Leviticus 1:3 - *If his offering be a burnt sacrifice of the herd, let him offer a male without blemish: he shall offer it of his own voluntary will at the door of the tabernacle of the congregation before the LORD.*

Leviticus 1:4 - *And he shall put his hand upon the head of the burnt offering; and it shall be accepted for him to make atonement for him.*

Leviticus 1:5 - *And he shall kill the bullock before the LORD: and the priests, Aaron's sons, shall bring the blood, and sprinkle the blood round about upon the altar that is by the door of the tabernacle of the congregation.*

Leviticus 1:6 - *And he shall flay the burnt offering, and cut it into his pieces.*

Leviticus 1:7 - *And the sons of Aaron the priest shall put fire upon the altar, and lay the wood in order upon the fire:*

Leviticus 1:8 - *And the priests, Aaron's sons, shall lay the parts, the head, and the fat, in order upon the wood that is on the fire which is upon the altar:*

Leviticus 1:9 - *But his inwards and his legs shall he wash in water: and the priest shall burn all on the altar, to be a burnt sacrifice, an offering made by fire, of a sweet savour unto the LORD.*

1. You will discover from the third verse of this passage that any 'offerer' was to do so willingly. Correspondingly, worship is a voluntary offering of our adulation to God. It is meant to be a natural flow of love from humanity to divinity. God compels no one to worship him.

2. Still in the same verse, the offerer was to present an animal without blemish. Worship is to ooze as pure myrrh from our hearts and lips, saturating and satisfying God as an acceptable aromatic-offering. He loves worship from an honest and pure heart. With out blemish!

3. The bullock was killed, its blood sprinkled on the altar and body parts cut in pieces and laid thereon. Implying that worship in its entirety entails sacrifice. It's an out pouring of a life of thanks and praise to God; for everything and in everything we go through and experience. In worship we come broken before him, laying our lives (like the body parts of an ox) on the altar of mercy and grace, acknowledging that we are finite and expendable. He is always interested in 'all' of us!

4. The eighth verse says, "the priest laid the parts in order on the fire upon the altar." Worship is an orderly account

of our magnification; a steady and systematic portrayal of a reverential life , driven by the fierily zeal of our love for God. Inferring that in times of worship we work our way into the bosom of the Father. God is never rushed! The atmosphere we build helps us move from the outer court of our flesh into the holy of H is presence. On our way in AND up, we lay memorial stones of thanksgiving depictive of a life's journey of faith and love. Additionally, the fire on the altar played a key role in consuming the sacrifice. This fire is the zeal of our hearts that should not at any one time be left to burn out. It is our vehement desire!

5. I personally like a well made steak. Its brownish appearance and scent makes me savor more. In like manner, a wholly devoted and sacrificial life, poured out on the altar of worship, is representative of sweet aroma/ incense to God. It makes God crave for more and more of it. That is why the scriptures say, "He seeks such to worship him"!

Chapter three

FACE OF A MAN

One of the cherubim had the face of a man. In scripture man is depicted as God's representative on the earthly realm, granted authority and power to administer it. In the book of Genesis, we see this stewardship entrusted to Adam. In this sphere, he exercises dominion. Accordingly, God will only intervene in the affairs of man on earth when his co-ruler invokes or invites him.

> **Psalms 115:16 -** *The heaven, even the heavens, are the LORD'S: but the earth hath he given to the children of men.*

In worship we exude this 'man-face' as we seek to invite

God into our affairs. Let us discover the mind of God about his greatest master piece...Man!

Psalms 8:4 - *What is man, that thou art mindful of him? and the son of man, that thou visitest him?*

Psalms 8:5 - *For thou hast made him a little lower than the angels, and hast crowned him with glory and honour.*

Psalms 8:6 - *Thou madest him to have dominion over the works of thy hands; thou hast put all things under his feet:*

Psalms 8:7 - *All sheep and oxen, yea, and the beasts of the field;*

Psalms 8:8 - *The fowl of the air, and the fish of the sea, and whatsoever passeth through the paths of the seas.*

Psalms 8:9 - *O LORD our Lord, how excellent is thy name in all the earth!*

By understanding your value and worth as 'regenerate-man', worship will elevate and make you realize your rightful position. The fourth verse is not silent about God being mindful of and desirous to visit man. He continuously seeks fellowship and friendship with us. Moments of worship help us draw close to him and he in turn draws close to us. The deep within us calls to the deep in him. This cultivates a bond of fellowship and friendship that matures every time we endeavor to wear our 'adoration-suits'. He becomes eager and anticipative of meeting with us. The consistent position of worship warrants us a 're-served seat' in the bosom of the father...glory to God!

Continuing our discussion with the fifth verse, worship will naturally attract glory and honor because these spontaneously ooze from the king. It is like walking through an abattoir, one can easily tell where you are coming from. "What flows from, flows out." In an ideal environment of his presence, worshippers will leave with a spiritual scent galvanized on them.

The sixth verse has two sections. One speaks of entrusting dominion over the works of His hands, the other putting all things under man's feet. Dominion/rulership is delegated authority. The next section relates to the power that subjects all under his feet. Power is ability entrusted. Authority is the right to exercise that ability. Eventually glory and honor are the benefits accruing to this elevated status of Man above God's other creations.

Two thousand years ago, 'regenerated-man' in Christ regained his lost position of power and authority. In worship, we are given leeway to exercise this authority and power to control and harness what has been assigned , above, beneath and on the earth's surface.

The scriptures say he has mandated us to pull down, destroy, build and plant. We are able to greatly influence the dark forces trying to manipulate the sphere of our government, whether they pass through the seas, in the air or on land. Ultimately, our worship will dethrone them and establish divine order and semblance in, through and about us. This is our jurisdiction. We ought to arise and utilize one of the greatest weapons of our warfare.... worship!

2 Kings 3:15 - *But now bring me a minstrel. And it came to pass, when the minstrel played, that the hand of the LORD came upon him.*

Furthermore, worship releases God to intervene in human affairs, as He treads and tames the spiritual and natural forces and makes us taste of nature's benefits. Remember, our God is a man of war , always waiting for his sons and daughters to invoke him to strike. At the same time, creation has been groaning waiting for the manifestation of his Sons. Worship is a tool that corrects satanic chaos . It makes our God go into pre-emptive attack mode. That is why the facial component of Man on the cherubim speaks volumes about our worship-position. Our creator wants us to eat the things naturally intended for us and to enjoy the good of the land.

Saints, let us awake individually and corporately and ascend to the mount of worship, fixing the groaning within and without as we endeavor to redeem our generation!

Chapter Four

FACE OF AN EAGLE

The eagle is considered king of the bird kingdom , master of the air. In some communities it is venerated as the messenger of the highest gods, in others it serves as a great symbol on flags and currencies. Mythologically, it is connected by the Greeks with the god Zeus and by the Romans with Jupiter. In primeval times of the mighty Roman empire, the eagle was engraved on their shields. It symbolized strength, courage, farsightedness and immortality.

There are substantial facts about an eagle that can help contextualize it in worship. The eagle speaks of Sensitiv-

ity and Excellence . The fourth cherub had the face as of a flying eagle. Let us compare and relate biblical evidence with natural phenomena.

1.Eagles fly alone and at high altitudes no other bird can attain. Eagles only fly with eagles.

> **Proverbs 23:5 -** *Wilt thou set thine eyes upon that which is not? for riches certainly make themselves wings; they fly away as an eagle toward heaven.*

Worship is a personal encounter with God, cultivated in the high realms of the spirit. As much as God is Omnipresent, his presence and glory are a 'gem' we should be willing to pursue. Like eagles, we are to soar via our worship above any familiar and natural surroundings that are occasional encumbrances to us to an elevated place in God. In this place of quietness and seclusion, we encounter God. Worship is a pursuit of excellence, taking us from glory to glory, from one dimension to another; enabling us tap into the infinite Jehovah.

> **Isaiah 8:17 -** *And I will wait upon the LORD, that*

hideth his face from the house of Jacob, and I will look for him.

Isaiah 45:15 - *Verily thou art a God that hidest thyself, O God of Israel, the Saviour.*

2. Eagles have strong vision which focuses up to five kilometers from the air. When it its spots prey, it will not lose sight of it in spite of any obstacle in its way.

Job 39:29 - *From thence she seeketh the prey, and her eyes behold afar off.*

Worship is a focused quest for God; that purposely ignores any obstacles to venerate Him and bask in His glory. In our life's journey, we are beset with circumstances that cause us lose sight of God. In this scenario, our natural instinct is to wallow and grapple. The eagle on spotting its kill will against all odds (blizzard, hurricane, etc) maintain its focus until it is accomplished.

As spiritual eagles, in our worship, we purpose to steady our mental, emotional and spiritual faculties on God in

spite of any existing pitfalls and downfalls. In magnifying HIM, we are demystifying our obstacles. We are consequently able to attain to our promises. Having spiritual sensitivity with consistent focus is key to hitting our mark!

3. Eagles, unlike vultures, do not eat dead things; they feed on fresh prey.

> **Job 9:26** - *They are passed away as the swift ships: as the eagle that hasteth to the prey.*

What an awesome natural principle! Yesterday's victory is not a guarantee for today's security. Many a Christian gets caught up in the spoils of the past and forgets that the battle still rages. By contrast, worship is our daily 'menu of love' served fresh to God for his goodness, grace and greatness. God enjoys fresh praise. He inhabits the praises of his people. The 'incense altar' of our heart should be kept aflame every day, cleared of the ashes of yesterday's sacrifice. Our Lord's prayer kick starts with praise and ends in adoration. Each day that

comes and goes should be packaged with a fresh serving
of a heart-love-feast for God. There is many a thing to
thank him for; what is already done, being done, going
to be done and what has not been done as well. When
God feeds, he is satiated and ready to fight for his child!

Hebrews 13:15 - *By him therefore let us offer the
sacrifice of praise to God continually, that is, the
fruit of our lips giving thanks to his name.*

4. The eagle is only bird that loves the storm. It uses the
storm to soar and glide by riding on it. Other birds will
scurry away in the leaves and branches of trees.

Proverbs 30:18 - *There be three things which are
too wonderful for me, yea, four which I know not:*

Proverbs 30:19 - *The way of an eagle in the air;
the way of a serpent upon a rock; the way of a ship
in the midst of the sea; and the way of a man with a
maid.*

Worship uses life's storms as norms for change. In worship, we learn to commemorate God, NOT condemn him. When Job lost everything, he fell down, tore his clothes and worshipped. His wife responded, curse God! Like other birds scurrying away in trees are countless Christians who, when they envisage a problem, hastily murmur, complain and castigate God for the happenings.

The eagle will use the occurrence to glide, by riding on the storm. Worship brings us to a place where we cease the hustle and bustle. We stop flapping our 'wings' and use the predicament as anchorage for adoration endeavoring to see God in and through the situation, knowing that he who brought us to, will bring us through.

> **Acts 16:23 -** *And when they had laid many stripes upon them, they cast them into prison, charging the jailor to keep them safely:*

> **Acts 16:24 -** *Who, having received such a charge, thrust them into the inner prison, and made their feet fast in the stocks.*

Acts 16:25 - *And at midnight Paul and Silas prayed, and sang praises unto God: and the prisoners heard them.*

5. The eagle has the longest life span of its species. It can live up to 70 years. However, when it reaches 40 years, its long and sharp beak becomes blunt; its old wings stick to its chest and makes it hard to fly. Either it dies OR goes through a process lasting 150 days. It flies to a mountain top, sits on its nest and knocks its beak on a rock till it plucks it out. It will wait for a new beak to grow, then it plucks out its talons. After new talons are grown it begins plucking out its old aged feathers. During that time it plucks out all the feathers on its body till it is bare. After five months the eagle takes its flight of rebirth and lives for another 30 years.

Micah 1:16 - *Make thee bald, and poll thee for thy delicate children; enlarge thy baldness as the eagle; for they are gone into captivity from thee.*

Psaims 103:5 - *Who satisfieth thy mouth with good things; so that thy youth is renewed like the eagle's.*

Our physical lives constitute emotions and a mind, all wrapped in this 'human tent.' In the course of our earthly pilgrimage, we encounter many challenges pre and post our salvation experience that occasion sin. The only place we can look to and run is the cross!

Worship is a lifetime school of transition; constantly bringing us to a place of shedding AND mending. Just as the eagle reaching its fortieth year resolves whether to die or go through a life change, we also as living stones are being built up to offer spiritual sacrifices acceptable to God. The more we cultivate the presence of God through worship, the more we behold and experience his majesty. This in turn reveals our sheer humanity, faults and need of his mercy and grace.

The process of shedding then comes into play. We begin 'offloading' as we admit our faults, habits, weaknesses, pains and pressures. These are reminiscent of the eagle's old beak, blunt talons and old/worn feathers. It is a painful and humbling process but mandatory for the next phase of our flight through the 'spiritual stratosphere'. This may take seasons of searching, loneliness and 'drought'; but a true seeker heart tempered with ado-

ration and deep reverence lessens the struggle on God's surgery table!

When the shedding is complete, God begins the mending process in us. The growth of a new beak, new talons and feathers is characteristic of a rebirth, new wine, new levels, new heights, etc. Our new lives and experience open us to a totally different spectrum in understanding God. The presence of God becomes more meaningful and tangible. From that moment on, we take our maiden flight of worship, filled with greater experiences of mercy and grace. For a Knowledge so priceless one will be willing to venture deeper.

For of him, and through him, and to him, are all things: to whom be glory forever. Amen. (Romans 11:36).

6. Eagles build their nests high on a cliff in a crevice where no predator is able to reach. The male and female participate in nest building.

Job 39:27 - *Doth the eagle mount up at thy command, and make her nest on high?*

Job 39:28 - *She dwelleth and abideth on the rock, upon the crag of the rock, and the strong place.*

One characteristic thing with eagles is that the female and male partner in nest building. Nesting denotes a new season in the cycle of this bird. It is a time to multiply! The nest is prepared in expectation of young eaglets. The two 'comrades' will take turns in the hatching process of the eggs. Similarly, worship elevates you to a place of dreaming and birthing great things. It is breeding ground for dreams and visions. When God dwells in our worship, he helps us birth greatness.

During those moments of intense spiritual intercourse with God, goals and dreams are birthed. We come to a place where God entrusts us with secrets and purposes for our lives. The deep in us begins calling to the deep in God. And the more we cultivate this intensity of fellowship, the more our 'eggs' are 'incubated' in his presence. The scripture says, "God inhabits the praises of his people". He broods over our dreams and helps see them turn into reality. Since worship is ideally a pursuit of God, with the ultimate stop being his throne, we are able to access a

measure of his mind and will for our lives.

The secret is being and maintaining this vigil. Just as the sequence of nest building takes time, so is our time of waiting and fellowship for the greater good. In worship, we are multiplied because you can never out give God. He is Jehovah Jireh!

Four Faces of a Worshipper

Chapter Five

EMBODIMENT

The four faces of the cherubim make each a masterpiece before their creator. As I have discussed in the preceding chapters, each of these faces and forms speaks volumes. The heart of God is seeing his greatest invention, Man, having the deepest fellowship with him. My prayer for us all is that in our generation, the good Lord will raise an army of worshippers who are a physical embodiment of the cherubim; that in every church and home, from pent house to white house, across continents and cultures, there will be a lifting up of holy hands in sincere reverence to God and as a result revivals will spring forth.

For where genuine worship is, there cannot but be a witnessing of God's love to an un-churched world. This will lead us to spontaneously and willingly leave our 'water-pots' and run to our Samarias saying, "Come see a Man who told me all that I ever did. " Soldier, it's time to rise up and size up. There is a trumpet call preparing us for an onslaught. A mighty wave of worship is about to hit the Church. Are you willing to venture into it?

BOOKS WRITTEN

1. Four Faces of a Worshipper
2. Worship Keys for Worthful living

COMING SOON

1. Gates of Worship
2. Nine Elements of Worship
3. Composition of Worship
4. Principles of Faith
5. Seven Locks of the Anointing
6. Seven Stages of Prayer
7. Seven Significances of the Cross
8. Art of Prayer

www.ingramcontent.com/pod-product-compliance
Lightning Source LLC
Chambersburg PA
CBHW060725030426
42337CB00017B/3011